American Bulldogs

Complete Owners Guide

By Joshua Brandon

Foreword

Although I am a great fan of the American Bulldog, I must say from the start that this is not a "beginner's dog" or the correct pet for anyone who cannot assert himself or herself as the "leader of the pack."

It's one thing to let yourself be pushed around by a small terrier or a Chihuahua. You may have a little ankle biter on your hands and a dog that has to be snatched up and controlled around other small dogs, but at least you *can* pick him up.

It's quite another matter to have an out of control guardian dog that can reach 150 lbs. (68 kg) and more in size. Aggression is a real possibility with this breed, and one you cannot sweep under the rug. These dogs are also incredibly stubborn and can be hard to control when excited.

That being said, part of the appeal of the breed that I personally enjoy is that very need for dedicated interaction and training. American Bulldogs are wonderfully loyal and affectionate. If you do your part, and offer your dog the early socialization and appropriate obedience training, you will enjoy a richly rewarding relationship with a highly intelligent dog.

The American Bulldog is handsome, muscular, and thoroughly athletic. They can be incredibly protective of children, but they're not babysitters, a fact I reiterate in the text. You must teach children how to behave appropriately with the dog, and you should supervise all interaction.

I do not recommend keeping an American Bulldog in a house with cats, or with smaller breeds. Tragedy typically ensues.

Generally it is best to engage the services of a professional trainer to educate both you and your new pet and to help you successfully establish your pack leadership.

At the end of this book, if you decide the American Bulldog is not the pet for you, I hope you will at least come away from the reading with a new respect for the breed. Sadly, many outstanding breeds have been tarred with the same brush used to vilify Pit Bulls. The American Bulldog is one of those dogs.

This blanket indictment is both erroneous and unfair as I hope you will come to understand as I attempt to introduce you to the mind and behavior of a truly unique breed.

Acknowledgments

To all the beautiful Bulldogs that have enriched our lives

Table of Contents

Table of Contents

Chapter 1 – History of the American Bulldog

The American Bulldog's true ancestors were mastiffs from Asia brought to England as early as 800 B.C. and bred by the native Celts to catch wild boar and cattle. Crossed with another mastiff, the Alaunt, that appeared in England around 400 A.D., the medieval English Bulldog was used to catch boar, cattle, and horses with its lock jaw grip.

These sturdy working dogs grasped the animals by the nose and refused to let go. Typically domestic livestock quickly submitted to the pain of the bite, with even large bulls lowering their heads to the ground and allowing themselves to be led to the slaughter.

This use of the dogs as well as staged competitions called "baits," continued into the 18th century Industrial Revolution.
Immigrants from the West Midlands of England settled

much of the American South. These groups brought their working dogs with them to their new homes. By modern standards, those animals were not a specific breed, but were simply of a bulldog "type."

Breeding considerations were based purely on dependability at tasks like guarding the farm, and often just on the availability of a dog of the opposite gender.

For these reasons, it's hard to pin down the exact origin of the American Bulldog, but we do know that he's a capable fellow who has never been averse to getting his paws dirty doing his appointed tasks.

By World War II, the bulldog "type" dogs that had dealt efficiently with feral hogs in the American South since the earliest days of settlement had all but disappeared except for individuals living in scattered sites across the region. An enthusiast, John D. Johnson, and his father set out to find the best surviving specimens.

Aided by a young man named Alan Scott, the Johnson's revitalization program met with considerable success, but eventually Scott's interest turned toward developing a leaner built dog now known today as the Standard American Bulldog.

Johnson, on the other hand, crossed his dogs with English bulldogs to improve the breed's strength and conformation. Consequently, he developed the Bully American Bulldog with its trademark burly, muscular build.

Still known around the world as "hog dogs," American Bulldogs are now a vigorous and thriving breed, not only working to catch escaped pigs and hunt feral hogs, but also as cattle dogs and canine athletes. They excel in sports requiring obedience, agility, and strength.

> **Tip**: In trying to explain the difference between the American Bulldog and pit bulls, emphasize that the American Bulldog is descended from mastiffs, while pit bull "types" are descended from crossing terriers and British bulldogs. American Bulldogs are much larger, have shorter snouts, and looser, more wrinkled facial skin.

Confusion with Pit Bulls

American Bulldogs are not "pit bulls," a term often applied to multiple breeds including American Staffordshire terriers, American pit bull terriers, and Staffordshire bull terriers.

The phrase "pit bull" now has a pejorative connotation associated with viciousness, attacks on humans, and organized dog fighting. Through no fault of their own, American Bulldogs are often lumped in with these breeds and equally vilified if for no other reason than they do have a resemblance to the pit bull types to people who do not know how to distinguish their unique differences.

Although American Bulldogs are capable of aggressive behavior if not appropriately trained, when well socialized and in the hands of a competent master, they are some of the best behaved dogs living in companionship with man. Even in the United States, there are different registration designations for dogs of the pit bull type. The United Kennel Club (UKC) registers them as "American Pit Bulls," but the American Kennel Club calls the breed "American Staffordshire Terriers."

In truth, the two groups of dogs have widely divergent ancestry. Pit bull "types" are descended from crossing terrier breeds with British bulldogs. American Bulldogs are derived from various types of mastiff. One of the greatest differences in these often-confused breeds is simply size.

- The American Pit Bull, according to the UKC standard, should stand 20 inches / 50.8 cm at the shoulder.

- The American Staffordshire Terrier, according to the AKC, stands 17-19 inches / 43.18-48.26 cm at the shoulder.

- The AKC measurement for the Staffordshire Bull Terrier is 14-16 inches / 35.56-40.64 cm.

American Bulldogs are considerably larger than all of these dogs, potentially weighing twice as much as any of these breeds and standing 20-27 inches / (50-71 cm) at the shoulder.

Another key area of difference is the conformation of the animals' head and snout. Pit bull "types" have a snout the equal to the length of or slightly longer than their skulls when seen from the side.
American Bulldogs have skulls longer than their snouts.

Looked at in profile from the skull to the snout, the skull should account for 55-80 percent of the distance.

Additionally, American Bulldogs have looser, more wrinkled facial skin, especially around the mouth, whereas pit bulls have taught skin and little if any wrinkling elsewhere on the head.

Guard Dog or Watch Dog?

A guard dog is an animal that can both face up to and confront an intruder. Such dogs possess both confidence and physical strength.

Watchdogs, on the other hand, simply alert their owners of an intruder's presence. They must have good hearing and a high level of intelligence. One of the best watchdogs is actually one of the smallest, the Chihuahua.

American Bulldogs are guard dogs. They have no difficulty confronting intruders, and in fact must be taught not to do so. There is no greater challenge presented by this breed than the absolute requirement for early socialization and solid obedience training that clearly establishes the owner as the master and pack leader.

It is a serious mistake to allow an American Bulldog to think he is the one in control.

Ignoring their guarding instinct is not natural for this breed. It's rather like asking a retriever *not* to chase a ball. The lesson not to guardcan and must be taught, but it requires contentious effort on the part of the dog's owner. If you are not prepared to make that commitment to mutual education and training, this is not the breed for you.

American Bulldog Physical Characteristics

As a consequence of the breed's evolution in modern times, the American Bulldog is a stocky animal with such dense musculature they easily execute vertical jumps of more than 7 feet / 2.13 meters.

Keeping a determined American Bulldog inside an enclosure requires a sturdy, *tall* fence!

Male Standards range in weight from 70-120 lbs. (30-58 kg) with Bullies being somewhat larger, 85-130 lbs. (38.5-59 kg), while all females are 60-90 lbs. (27.2-40.8 kg).

Males stand 20-27 inches at the shoulder (50-71 cm); females 20-24 inches (50.8-61 cm).

The short, harsh coat is white with varying patches of red and brindle or fawn and brindle. The breed is classed as working dogs and guardians. Lifespan is typically 10-15 years.

American Bulldog Organizations

The parent canine organizations in the United States and the United Kingdom are the American Kennel Club and The Kennel Club. Typically these are the groups that formulate the accepted breed standards for showing specific animals and are the sponsoring bodies of dog shows.

- Since it was founded in 1884, **The American Kennel Club** has promoted purebred dogs and worked on behalf of their welfare as an advocate for responsible ownership and canine health.

   The AKC maintains an extensive registry of purebred dogs as a means of identification and verification of pedigree. You can see the organization's website at: www.akc.org.

- **The Kennel Club**, founded in 1873, promotes the health and welfare of all dogs. The organization also sets the rules for conducting sporting field trials and showing dogs. The website for the group is www.thekennelclub.org.uk.

American Bulldog specific groups include:

American Bulldog Association
www.american-bulldog.com

American Bulldog Rescue
www.americanbulldogresuce.org

Federation American Bulldog
www.federationab.com

The Bulldog Club of America Rescue Network
www.rescuebulldogs.org

American Bulldog EU
abeu.eu/en

ABRA - American Bulldog Registry & Archives
www.abra1st.com

There are also many fine regional and local dog clubs that are dedicated wholly or in part to the American Bulldog breed. One of the best ways to find such organizations is to attend a dog show in your area.

Note: *At this writing in mid-2014 all of the above sites were active, but like all things on the Internet, I can make no future guarantees of their availability.*

Chapter 2 – Before Buying an American Bulldog

The American Bulldog is an active working dog found in two types, the "Bully" and the "Standard." As the name would imply, Bullies are stocky, muscular dogs with large, powerful heads while Standards are more elongated and athletic.

The breed is known for its protective personality and extreme loyalty to its "pack." While a good family dog that will tolerate children – and even show great affection toward them – the American Bulldog requires early socialization. Owners must understand how the dog sees the world and what he perceives his role to be within the family.

A well-trained American Bulldog is an excellent pet, but only in partnership with a dedicated master.

Male or Female?

The decision to purchase a male or female American Bulldog puppy is an important one. You are not just deciding boy or girl based on the usual factors that one considers when selecting any other puppy. The personality, behavior, and protective instincts of your new family member are greatly determined by gender.

Female American Bulldogs make the best family companions due to the decreased risk of aggression and the breed's reputation for solid maternal instincts including patience and tolerance with young children.

If you do adopt a male, the dog should definitely be altered before he reaches one year of age. Medically, this is the best phase of life for the surgery to be performed, and behaviorally, it helps to preempt incidents of aggression.

One or Two?

Although American Bulldogs can make fine family dogs, it is typically best to adopt only one. The risk for aggressive behavior is too great with multiples, and the dogs demand a great deal from their owners in terms of time, attention, and commitment to training.

Weighing the Pros and Cons

It is always difficult to arrive at lists of "pros" and "cons," but in a world that favors boiling things down to bullet lists, this is always the kind of summary approach readers seem to want.

Please bear in mind, however, that what is a positive in the eyes of one person may be a negative for another. Always weigh breed choice and the overall wisdom of adopting a pet purely in the context of your life and personal preferences, needs, and tolerances.

Reasons in Favor of the American Bulldog

- Muscular, powerful breed well suited to an active, athletic life.

- Imposing in appearance, but good-natured with

people when well trained and appropriately socialized.

- Thrives on close bonding, training, and time with his master.

- Sleek coat with minimal grooming needs.

Reasons Against the American Bulldog

- A relatively large dog that needs space.

- Can be resistant to housebreaking.

- Has a need for vigorous exercise.

- Rowdy and exuberant and prone to jumping.

- Requires socialization to curb a protective instinct.

- Can be aggressive with people and other animals.

- Strong-willed and stubborn.

- Needs a confident "in charge" owner.

Potential Legal Issues

You must also be prepared to accept widespread negative public perception. Many people who see your American Bulldog will immediately think "pit bull." This has far greater potential ramifications than someone just not "liking" your dog. It can generate insurance headaches and start real problems with your neighbors.

Homeowners Insurance

You face the risk of insurance problems, struggles with your homeowners association, and the difficulty of breed specific bans. Through no fault of the dog's, he may well be a legal liability for you under the wrong circumstances.

Although insurance "blacklists" for breeds vary widely, the 14 dogs most commonly singled out include:

- Pit Bull Terriers
- Staffordshire Terriers
- Rottweilers
- German Shepherds
- Presa Canarios
- Chows Chows
- Doberman Pinschers
- Akitas
- Wolf-hybrids
- Mastiffs
- Cane Corsos
- Great Danes
- Alaskan Malamutes
- Siberian Huskies

While the American Bulldog isn't on this list, he is often mistaken, as I have said, for a pit bull or a pit bull "type."

Be prepared to have to defend your dog if a homeowners insurance issue arises. And be prepared to lose. Dogs and dog owners don't often fare well in such confrontations.

Homeowners Associations

It is also possible that a homeowners association may object to the keeping of a breed it believes to be dangerous on appearance alone. HOAs have gained a reputation for being Draconian in their tactics and are driving forces behind many "breed specific" laws and ordinances.

Such groups can be absolutely intractable in their refusal to understand breed differences or to evaluate animals on their individual history and behavior.

Address These Problems Before Adopting

You would be well advised to investigate all of these concerns **before** you bring an American Bulldog into your life. Failure to do so is frankly highly irresponsible on your part and completely unfair to the dog.

In the end, the dog is the one that will suffer the most from such legal and procedural squabbling. American Bulldogs become so attached to their owners that rehoming this breed is problematic at best.

Attempting to do so often brings out the aggressiveness that people fear in the first place. It is a sad fact that in most animal shelters and non-breed specific rescue groups, dogs labeled aggressive are simply euthanized.

Do not be guilty of placing an innocent dog's life in jeopardy by failing to investigate or openly flaunting insurance, legal, or association-based requirements that you were aware of in advance.

An animal lover's primary consideration should always be the welfare of the animal, even if that means you must decide that adopting a pet or this breed in particular is not the right choice given your current circumstances.

Chapter 3 – American Bulldog Personality

No matter how attractive you may find the American Bulldog, or how much you are drawn to the athletic nature of the breed, this is not the dog for everyone. No breed should be adapted on a whim, especially this one.

One of the greatest challenges you will face is the reaction other people have to your dog. Because the American Bulldog is often confused with the pit bull, many people will stiffen or tense up around your pet. Never underestimate your dog's ability to sense the emotion, but do question his ability to interpret it correctly.

It cannot be said often enough. The American Bulldog is a *guardian breed*. If an untrained dog senses fear and apprehension in another person, you face one of two possible outcomes. His prey drive may be activated, which could cause aggression toward the weaker party, or he could decide the other human or animal is poised for attack.

American Bulldogs are social pack animals. They need an alpha to guide their decisions and actions. That alpha must be you. Otherwise, the dog's guardian instincts, which seem perfectly reasonable and natural to him, may get you both in a great deal of trouble.

Energetic and Agile

American Bulldogs are incredibly energetic and agile. They need to be with someone who has the time to interact with them, not just in play and horsing around, but also in serious training and conditioning. If you're not reasonably fit yourself, you're going to have a very hard time keeping up with this dog!

Exercise is necessary for an American Bulldog to stay physically fit and trim, but the breed also needs adequate activity to remain emotionally well balanced. While any dog likes quiet time, an American Bulldog won't loll around all day waiting for you to come home and then take a leisurely stroll around the block.

Think of bringing an American Bulldog into your life as acquiring a new partner, one that will be with you 10 years or longer. Ideally, you should have a clear sense of where you will be and how you will be living for at least a decade when you adopt this breed.

They are wonderfully versatile dogs that enjoy and do well with training, but they want to be with their owner – doing, doing, *doing*! You should have a fenced yard, both to give your pet a safe place to exercise and to keep him contained for his own protection. Good fences also help to control potential aggressive interactions with other dogs.

Highly Dominant

If you've never raised a teenager, you're about to – one with four paws, a real dominant streak, and a highly intelligent mind capable of making an independent decision. American Bulldogs, however, are so instinct driven, they don't always make choices we would consider right or "good." If you let your young dog bully you, the precedent will be set for having a mature but uncontrollable dog.

Unless you firmly establish yourself as the leader of the "pack," you could have an animal that will be aggressive with other dogs and people (especially strangers), which is *not* a good situation.

> **Tip:** When a visitor, especially someone "new" comes to your home, you should greet the person and shake his hand first. Don't let the person approach your pet before they interact with you.
>
> American Bulldogs take their cues from their owner, who should also be the "pack leader." If it is clear to your dog that you are relaxed and in charge and the person that has just entered your "territory" is not an intruder, there should be no triggering of the dog's protective instinct.

In handling any dog, you should never confuse good discipline with punishment. The point of sound dog training is to channel the animal's natural instincts into acceptable behaviors. It is highly likely you will need help from a professional trainer to accomplish this balance.

Socialization is Imperative

Socialization in a variety of settings is crucial to create the clear perception in your pet's mind that other dogs are not enemies and that people are not intruders. This approach does not negate the protective instincts of the breed, but rather teaches the dog to take his cues from you. If you are truly threatened at home or while you are out with your dog, you can be assured an American Bulldog will stand up for his master.

You simply have to make sure the dog can accurately read the situation based on your demeanor and follow the commands you give him. If you are prepared for this level of interaction and involvement with a companion canine, then the American Bulldog can be an absolutely exceptional family dog or a best friend for a single person.

The breed is active and confident by nature, but they also have emotional personalities that require active attention on the part of the humans with whom they bond strongly.

As puppies, expect the breed to be aloof with strangers, a tendency that will disappear with age. The key to raising a well-adjusted and well-controlled American Bulldog is to expose your pet to other dogs and to people at an early age both inside and out of the home.

Chapter 4 – American Bulldog Behavior

American Bulldogs can exhibit great affection toward children and in the vast majority of cases the dogs tend to be extremely protective. Be aware, however, that this breed has a strong prey drive, which can be activated by an overly excited child running and screaming.

Understanding the importance of the prey drive is fundamental in deciphering and controlling your dog's behavior. A great deal of the basis for effective training is anticipating how your dog will react and taking the appropriate steps in advance to prevent problems before they arise.

Understanding the Prey Drive

A "prey drive" is the instinct present in any type of carnivore (or omnivore, in the case of dogs) to chase and catch prey. This is a term that is used in dog training to analyze habits present in particular breeds.

Dog-related injuries and even fatalities are most often associated with children and the elderly. When a dog's prey instinct is activated, the animal is able to judge the likelihood that it will be able to defeat an "opponent" and will go after what it perceives to be weak.

The American Bulldog and Children

Frankly, the reviews are mixed on the behavior of American Bulldogs with children. The breed is capable of being very loving and with young kids, but can also react negatively in certain circumstances. The bottom line is that education on both sides of the equation is the best prevention.

The dog must be taught how to behave around children, but children must also understand how to behave around the dog. This includes such fundamentals as:

- Never approach any dog without the owner's permission even if you know the animal.

- Don't jump or yell at a sleeping dog or do anything else to startle the animal into action.

- Don't chase a dog that is trying to get away from you.

- Don't bother a dog while it's eating or playing with a bone or a chew toy.

- Do not make eye contact with a dog and stare at him for a long period of time. In dog language this is an open challenge.

- Don't play games that reinforce aggressive behavior, like "tug of war."

Teach children to interact gently with all animals and to recognize them as living creatures with feelings and emotional reactions. Even the gentlest family pet may lash out when they are in pain or afraid from being slapped, poked, squeezed or otherwise harassed.

Joint socialization of dogs and children is not a training option with American Bulldogs; it's a requirement. There is no substitute for close adult supervision with children and dogs. I cannot stress this point strongly enough -- ***dogs are not babysitters.***

Also, just because your dog is fine around your children you cannot take that as an accurate indicator of the animal's behavior around other children. The dog may even regard the strange children as a threat to your kids and act out accordingly.

With Other Animals

The American Bulldog often becomes aggressive with other dogs due both to its prey drive and the overall dominance of its personality. Often, you will have no idea what started the fight.

Dogs have a complex vocabulary built on body language. If an American Bulldog can't interpret clearly what another dog is "saying," he'll fight first and ask questions later.

With littermates and dogs they know well, American Bulldogs will rough house, but by age 1-2 years, the breed will fight viciously if provoked. This fact alone is a compelling reason to have males neutered.

This is not to suggest that females won't fight. Remember that American Bulldogs were bred to catch and bring down livestock and are excellent at hunting feral hogs. They are fearless when their natural instincts are fully activated.

Warning!

Use extreme caution keeping smaller dogs with an American Bulldog.

DO NOT try to have cats in the same household with this breed.

Puppy or Adult? Rehoming?

Optimistic new owners who over-estimated their ability to keep such an active, dominant, and headstrong breed as the American Bulldog give up their animals to rescue groups regularly. Nine times out of ten, these people have done no research into the breed before adopting.

This serious mistake leaves thousands of adult American Bulldogs without a home and sadly without a great deal of hope.

Like many guardian breeds, American Bulldogs are very hard to place or "re-home." If the dog has a documented reputation for aggression, he will likely be euthanized immediately.

Even more tragic is the fact that many potential "parents" take one look at the breed and assume they are aggressive regardless of the dog's history. This is such a standard reaction; some shelters don't even *try* to place these dogs. While I am an avid supporter of all canine rescue organizations, I cannot emphasize strongly enough that American Bulldogs are NOT for everyone.

Only highly experienced dog owners should even consider adopting this breed from a rescue situation. Even then, you must be very discriminating and demand full discloser about the dog's previous behavior.

No matter how much experience you may have in dealing with aggressive and protective breeds like the American Bulldog, if you are considering adopting an adult, you MUST know the animal's history.

It is also important to have the dog evaluated by a qualified dog trainer to judge his suitability to come into your home. Do not regard this suggestion as an over-reaction.

Experts know how to place just enough stress on a dog to judge his likely reactions under a variety of circumstances and with different types of people, but in controlled conditions where no harm will come either to the people he encounters or to the animal himself.

Pick a Puppy a Family Pet

For family pets, your best course of action is to adopt a puppy and to ensure that the animal is appropriately trained for life as a companion.

This is the only truly safe option, especially if you have

children in the home. Early positive socialization helps an American Bulldog realize its full potential as a companion animal.

This is not to imply that the American Bulldog is not an exceptional dog in his own right; he is. But his qualities must be channeled and cultivated. These are hardheaded and somewhat high strung dogs.

Beginning with a puppy gives you the best possible chance to mold your new pet's behavior into the correct level of interaction for your lifestyle and circumstances.

Chapter 5 – Purchasing an American Bulldog

The reputation dogs have for being man's best friend also makes them profitable commodities for unscrupulous "breeders." Being able to recognize the difference between a legitimate kennel with verifiable bloodlines, and a scam is the first step in purchasing your new pet.

Avoiding Scams and Puppy Mills

Profit is the only reason for a puppy mill to exist. The crooks who run these operations want to spend as little as possible while charging high prices for dogs that have been born into substandard and often squalid conditions.

Little if any thought is given to genetic quality and early health care. With a breed as sensitive as the American Bulldog, the consequence can be not only a physically unhealthy animal, but also one with lifelong emotional and behavioral issues.

When you begin your search for a pedigreed American Bulldog, do NOT fall for "deals" that offer puppies at discounted prices in exchange for breeding the animal and surrendering the puppies back to the breeder. This is simply a variation of the "puppy mill" scheme that ensures these operations maintain a steady "inventory."

Such operations do business both online and off. They may suggest that in some way their dogs are unusual or "rare," or make spurious claims that there are no genetic defects in their "lines."

American Bulldogs are typically healthy animals with few genetic issues. This topic will be covered fully in the chapter on health, but for now, know that claims of genetic perfection are impossible with any breed and there are few reliable screening methods.

Most defects are detected only after the dogs are born. Provided the physical issue is not painful and debilitating, such animals are spayed or neutered and placed in good homes as companion animals.

Responsible kennels fight inherited disorders and physical defects with careful breeding programs and employ the screening methods that are available and have been judged to be reliable. Puppy mills take no such precautions and seek only to churn out as many litters as possible. Since puppy mills are often prime suppliers for pet shops, do not support such operations.

There are hundreds of thousands of wonderful dogs in need of a home. These groups have nothing but the dogs' best interests at heart and are doing everything possible to save their lives and avoid euthanizing unwanted animals.

When you are searching for a puppy if you cannot:

- visit the kennel
- meet the parents
- play with all the puppies
- inspect the facilities
- see registration papers
- and review health records

. . . do not buy a dog from the "breeder."

Locating and Dealing with a Breeder

If at all possible, find a local breeder or one in driving distance of your home. I am not in favor of shipping live animals and certainly not in the cargo hold of an airplane.

If you are considering purchasing a dog at a distance, factor travel costs for yourself into the total expense, including a ticket for your new pet to ride with you in the cabin on the return flight.

As you begin your search for a legitimate breeder, begin by asking for recommendations from your veterinarian or local dog club. If there is a dog show scheduled in your area, plan on attending.

While this is not the setting to actually adopt a dog, it's a great place to collect business cards and to get a good look at the dogs produced by any one kennel.

Plan on visiting each kennel in which you're interested in person. You not only want to talk about what's involved in adopting one of their dogs, but also tour the facility and learn about their breeding program.

> **Tip:** When you visit a kennel, you should receive a complete tour of the facility. If you don't have a sense that you are being dealt with in an open and honest way, you may not be dealing with a reputable breeder. Beware!

Reputable kennels have absolutely no problem showing people around, and most breeders will happily talk about their dogs day and night.

You're looking for an operation that is clearly friendly and open in their dealings, one where the dogs live with ample space in clean surroundings and clearly benefit from superior care and interaction.

There should always be a sense in your conversation with the breeder that information is free flowing. You should both ask and answer questions and there should be ample consideration of both the positive and negatives of life with an American Bulldog.

You want a breeder that is very enthusiastic about the breed, but who will also frankly discuss issues of aggression and the need for positive training and close bonding with the "pack leader."

Why "Pet Quality?"

The short answer to why buy a "pet quality" animal is, frankly, affordability. Show quality dogs from highly regarded kennels are well beyond the price point of someone looking for a companion animal.

It's important that you understand that there is nothing "less" associated with the term "pet quality." Kennels look at puppies from an early age and make a determination of their quality when judged against the accepted list of standards for the breed.

Animals that conform most closely to the breed standard go into breeding programs and are shown in exhibition. Those that do not are made available for adoption to good homes as pets with the provision that they be spayed or neutered within the first 6-12 months of life.

This requirement is made in the interest of maintaining the purity of the breed, protecting the kennel's carefully cultivated bloodlines, and stemming the tide of tragically unwanted companion animals.(As I have already mentioned, neutering males also decreases the risk of aggressive behavior.)

Truth be told, even when a breeder points out to you why a puppy is regarded as "pet quality" you probably won't be able to see the "problem." All you will see is an impossibly cute, exuberant dog ready and willing to become your best buddy.

Bad Breeders: The Signs

Understandably one of the greatest concerns expressed by people buying a pedigreed dog for the first time is, "How will I know if I'm working with a bad breeder?" Consider all of the following points as potential warning signs that something is not right.

- Reluctance on the part of the breeder or kennel owner to allow you to visit the facility in person. This might be expressed by saying, "I'll bring the puppy to you" or "we can just meet at . . ."

- An offer to sell a puppy to you sight unseen. For instance, "Just have the money ready and I'll bring a dog to you." There will also likely be evasiveness in regard to the fate of the littermates and the identity of the parents.

- Being allowed to visit the kennel, but not to see the whole facility. "Oh, we're doing some work back there" or "that's a private area."

- Over-crowded conditions with an obvious smell.

- Watch how the animals behave. If they are apprehensive and nervous beyond the bounds of typical puppy exuberance, be suspicious.

- Not being allowed to meet one or both of the puppies' parents. While it is common for the sire not to be present at the kennel, you should be able to meet the mother and to review the father's information as well as see a photograph.

- Inability to prove membership in a kennel club or claims of, "Oh, I don't bother joining those groups." This goes hands in hand with having no paperwork regarding pedigree or an ability to prove at least three generations of the dog's ancestry.

- Having no health information on the puppies or their parents along with claims that, "None of my dogs are ever sick." Also be suspicious if the breeder says, "I'll get the records and send them to you later."

- Assertions that the dog is micro chipped, but they have no scanner to prove this fact or to match up the ID number on the chip with the one entered on the bill of sale.

- Any dodgy behavior regarding the bill of sale, either claiming one is not needed or again, "I'll send that to you."

Also be highly suspicious of any adoption agreement that does not include some form of a health guarantee. The effectiveness of this assurance is usually contingent on the puppy being evaluated by a qualified veterinarian within a set period of time after adoption.

Good Breeders: The Signs

By the same token, you will know you're working with a good breeder if all of the following points are true.

- It is clear that the welfare of the dog is the deciding point in the negotiation. It may come as a shock, but breeders can and do turn down potential adoptions regardless of the money involved if they do not think the dog would be going to a good home.

- There's more than once chance to interact with the puppies and one or both of the parents. This is an important test to judge the temperament of the adult dogs and to see if there is one puppy in particular with which you bond. Many canine experts say the best way to pick a puppy is to let the little dog come to you.

- The breeder has registered the dog with a kennel club and chosen its official name. Proof of this fact is produced with an explanation of how the registration will be transferred from the breeder's name to your own.

- A full and informed discussion of the importance of socialization should occur, complete with advice on how to continue the program at home and recommendations of resources and professionals who can assist you with training your new pet.

Breeders who are concerned and involved with their animals do not see an adoption purely in business terms. They want to know where the puppies are going and how they will live. They will ask questions about you, your life and work, your family, and your schedule.

Don't be offended, and answer honestly. Remember you are talking with someone who knows American Bulldogs intimately and can give you sound advice on how well the dog will or won't adapt to your lifestyle.

I'd be far more worried about a breeder who doesn't ask these questions than one who does. I always want to work with someone who clearly is very passionate about the American Bulldog breed and has a serious interest in ensuring the dog's future health and happiness.

Materials the Breeder Will Provide

As part of the adoption process, there are certain items the breeder will supply. Make sure that all of your questions are fully answered and that you understand the explanations before proceeding with the transaction.

- **The contract.**

  The contract should contain a detailed explanation of what is expected of both parties in all aspects of the bill including payment, health checks, and transfer of registration papers.

  Be sure to go over all of the provisions of the contract with the breeder and do not sign the final document until you are sure you understand everything it contains.

- **Helpful information.**

  The breeder should supply you with useful information relative to the dog's transition from the kennel to your home. This should include material on diet, exercise, necessary health procedures (worming, vaccinations, spaying/neutering), and training.

Review this material and ask for any additional information that will be helpful to you, like making contact with a veterinarian, a trainer, or a groomer. Use the connection to the breeder to make the best start with your puppy possible!

- **The dog's pedigree.**

  You should receive a copy of the dog's pedigree or ancestry that goes back at minimum three generations. This may be in handwriting or supplied as an official copy from a governing kennel club. Regardless, there should be adequate detail to allow you to independently verify the dog's lineage.

- **Health records.**

  You should receive all existing health records for the puppy as well as any relevant health-related information about the parents. This will likely include what vaccinations the dog has already received and the proposed schedule of boosters.

  There should also be explanatory material about any potential genetic conditions associated with the breed. Ideally, the breeder will have discussed genetic issues with you in advance and explained how or if the animals in the kennel have been screened.

Honest breeders will tell you that in some cases there are no reliable tests for given conditions.

Typically there will be a statement regarding the dog's health and condition at the time of adoption along with a stipulated period during which a qualified veterinarian should examine the puppy. This provision serves to activate the broader terms of most health guarantees and should be accompanied by an explanation of what if any refund you will receive if the dog does fall ill.

ID Methods for Pedigree Dogs

The majority of pedigreed dogs are marked with some permanent means of identification. The American Kennel Club, for instance, advocates a "common sense" approach to the use of both tattoos and microchips.

The Kennel Club in the UK certifies dog breeders via the

Kennel Club Assured Breeder Scheme, which requires the use of a microchip, tattoo, or DNA profile as a means of permanent identification.

Additionally, dogs traveling to or returning to the UK from another country can do so under the Pet Passport system, which also necessitates micro chipping.

For more information see: www.gov.uk.take-pet-abroad

Approximate Purchase Price

Although prices always vary by region and kennel, most breeders offer pet quality American Bulldogs in the price range of $1400-$2000 / £815-£1165.

Chapter 6 –Life with an American Bulldog

The first step in welcoming an American Bulldog puppy into your life is to make your home safe for the little dog. The purpose of "puppy proofing" is twofold:

- removing potentially dangerous hazards that might cause the puppy harm and,

- safeguarding your possessions against the maniacal chewing urges of an endlessly curious, hyperactive young dog!

You can't engage in this process from 5 or 6 feet (1.52-1.82 meters) up in the air! Get down on your hands and knees, or on your belly, and have a look around from puppy level.

The things that catch your eye are the ones that need to be removed, tied down, tucked up, or otherwise secured. This could be anything from electrical cords to that torn bit of fabric on the corner of the sofa.

A determined American Bulldog could have all the upholstery off in the time it takes you to get a load of wash in the dryer!

Consider all such items from the perspective of multiple threats. A drapery pull will not only bring the curtains down, but it's a choking hazard. An electrical cord can cause electrocution, or topple over the TV set.

Think like a bored and inventive puppy and you'd be

surprised how much trouble there is to be made in any one room of your home.

Remember that puppies will chew on *anything*. Don't assume anything is safe – TV remotes, cell phones, chargers, iPads – get everything above puppy level and out of sight. American Bulldogs are *very good jumpers*.

Hazardous Substances

Many times puppies are initially secured in a kitchen or bathroom. Make sure that you use child locks on the doors and remove all potentially hazardous chemicals just in case.

Do the same with any houseplants since even those that are

not poisonous to dogs per se will often cause severe gastrointestinal upset.

As the dog is allowed more access to the house think about items like:

- cleaners
- detergents
- insecticides
- mothballs
- fertilizers
- antifreeze

In the event that your dog does get into something you think is toxic, take the following steps:

- Remove your pet from the area where the substance is present and make sure the material is secured so other pets and children are not in danger.

- Collect a sample of whatever the dog ate or chewed including any package or container that might contain useful ingredient information.

- Don't give the dog any of the old "home remedies" including milk, salt, oil, or any kind of food.

- Do nothing to induce vomiting (including administering hydrogen peroxide) unless directed to do so by a veterinarian or an expert at an animal poison hotline.

Get your dog to your vet or to an emergency animal hospital as soon as possible or call a poison hotline. Do not wait to see if the dog gets sicker. Act quickly!

In the United States, the American Association for the Prevention of Cruelty to Animals (ASPCA) maintains a number at (888) 426-4435.

In the United Kingdom, vets may call 020 7188 0200.

Buying Travel and Home Crates

You will need a large travel crate for your puppy. By 11 weeks, most American Bulldogs are already pushing 20 lbs. / 9.07 kg.

A crate that is rated for dogs weighing 20-30 lbs. / 9.07-13.60 kg is considered a "medium." The dimensions are typically 28" x 20" x 19" high / 71.12 cm x 50.8 cm x 48.26 cm. The price will be around $70 / £40.83.

(Since your dog will ultimately weigh anywhere from 60 lbs. / 27.2 kg to 130 lbs. / 59 kg, a crate will be impractical and the dog will graduate to a canine seatbelt for car trips.)

Crate training is highly recommended for American Bulldogs, so you will also need to purchase an appropriate wire crate for use in your home.

There is always a temptation to buy a huge crate for a young dog in an effort to save money. After all, he'll grow into it, right? Wrong!

The crate is an important part of housebreaking and if you give a puppy enough room, he'll choose a far corner and do his businesses right there – the very thing you're trying to avoid and teach him NOT to do.

Better to spend a little extra on an additional crate later later on than to go through a more protracted housebreaking process than is necessary.

A wire crate similar in size to the travel crate described above retails for around $50 / £30, with one size up selling for $60 / £35. The really big crates, rated for dogs weighing around 110 lbs. / 50 kg cost $85 to $100/ £50 to £58.

The First Trip Home

When transporting a puppy to its new home for the first time it's always a good idea to include an article of clothing you've worn in the crate along with some puppy-safe chew toys.

Remember that you are dealing with a young animal leaving the only home it has ever known. You want the dog to feel safe and to begin to know you by your scent. Always secure the crate in place with the seat belt and make sure the fit is snug.

Coordinate with the breeder so the dog has not eaten before the drive and that all of this "business" has been handled. Expect some whining and crying during the trip; it's completely normal.

If, however, you're looking at a very long drive, you may want to have someone along to help you by sitting with the dog and comforting it. Do not, however, remove the puppy from the crate while the car is in motion.

If you have children, no matter how much they want to come along, leave them at home. The transition from the kennel will be a stressful one for the puppy, and also confusing. You want the drive to be as calm and quiet as possible.

Upon arrival, let the dog relieve himself and encourage his good habits by praising him for going "outside." Housebreaking training should begin immediately and be based on a program of positive reinforcement.

Dogs have an inherent desire to please the leader of their "pack," which is greatly to your advantage with a breed as potentially headstrong as the American Bulldog.

Allow the dog undisturbed time to acclimate to his new surroundings in a contained area like a kitchen or bathroom, but make sure he can see you.

Use a baby gate if necessary to create a barrier, but remember, American Bulldogs grow quickly and they are very, very good jumpers.

Gates are also helpful to keep puppies away from stairs and other obstacles they might not yet be ready to negotiate

safely. Depending on the size and model, gates cost $25-
$100 / £14.87-£59.46.

The whining and crying is likely to continue, especially
during the first night. Take the puppy out to do his
"business" right before bedtime and then get the dog
settled in its crate.

Don't take him out of the crate until morning. He will calm
down and no, you're not the worst American Bulldog
parent in the world. Dogs will work you just like kids will.
Don't fall for it!

Canines derive a sense of security from their "den" and will
not soil it, so use of a crate is highly important in
housebreaking. Take the puppy out first thing in the
morning. Don't make him wait!

Routine Grooming

The short and somewhat harsh coat of the American
Bulldog is extremely easy to groom. They are not heavy
shedders and only require bathing every 30 to 60 days, a
task that can easily be accomplished in the bathtub with
warm water and a pet specific shampoo.

More frequent baths will only strip the coat of the natural
oils that provide its trademark sheen.

Bathing

When bathing your pet, take care that the shampoo does

not get in either the dog's eyes or ears. Shampoo from the neck down to the tail being sure to scrub all the areas where dirt can hide including skin crevices, between the toes, and under the tail.

Wipe the dog clean with a fluffy towel. In warm weather, let your pet go outside and shake off the excess, otherwise keep him inside until he's thoroughly dry.

Brushing

The more you brush the coat of an American Bulldog the more it glows with good health. Get a brush with soft bristles, testing it along the inside of your arm to make sure it won't scratch your pet's skin.

Brushing your dog once a day with a straight, backward motion will keep his coat sleek, shiny, and clean. Work from the head down to the tail, talking and praising your dog all the while. This is an excellent bonding time, and one your pet will enjoy enormously.

Managing Fleas And Ticks

Active outdoor dogs like the American Bulldog simply will pick up the stray flea and tick from time to time. This is not a calamity, and certainly something that is manageable if dealt with immediately and appropriately. Don't overreact! The dog hasn't done anything "bad!"

Puppies under 3 months of age should never be treated with any product containing pyrethrum. There have been adverse and even fatal reactions reported in small dogs, including long-term neurological damage.

In my opinion, a good bath followed by the use of a fine-toothed flea comb is still the best way to address flea eradication. The parasites become trapped in the teeth and die when the comb is submerged in hot soapy water.

All soft materials including bedding with which the dog has come into contact must also be washed in hot water daily until you are sure all the fleas and their eggs have been killed.

Over the same period, check the dog for live fleas and evidence of the dried blood they excrete. This "flea dirt" looks like little specks of gravel and tends to accumulate around the ears, in the armpits, and around the tail.

Remove ticks by coating them completely with petroleum jelly, which will clog their breathing holes. After about 5 minutes, wipe the jelly away with a paper towel.

Often the tick simply comes away as well, otherwise, gently remove the parasite with a smooth backward motion to make sure the head does not remain behind and cause a sore.

Nail Trimming

Typically American Bulldogs are active enough to wear their nails down either walking on rough surfaces or asphalt. If this is not the case, you will need to perform the chore yourself with a trimmer specifically designed for use with dogs.

The models that offer the greatest level of control have plier grips and retail for under $20 / £11.88. If you begin this chore early in your dog's life, you'll have no problem working with your pet regardless of his size.

Clip the tip of each nail at a 45-degree angle being careful to avoid the vascular quick at the base, which will bleed heavily if nicked. Keep a styptic stick or powder on hand in case this does happen.

Anal Glands

Dogs have two glands on either side of the anus that typically empty when the dog defecates. If, however, these anal glands become blocked and foul smelling, it will be necessary to express them, a sensitive chore to which many owners do not feel equal.

On a breed as large and potentially aggressive as the American Bulldog, I recommend that the animal's veterinarian or groomer handle this task. If done correctly, it is a fast and painless process.

Owners tend to be understandably tentative about this grooming necessity. If the dog picks up on your nervousness and lack of confidence, the chore is made unnecessarily unpleasant for all concerned.

Symptoms of clogged anal glands include scooting or

rubbing the bottom on the ground or carpet. If the glands are not expressed, a painful abscess can form.

Regular Exercise

Regular exercise is beneficial for all dogs, but a daily walk is especially good for your American Bulldog because it will expose him to a variety of sights, sounds, and smells. When your dog sees that you are confident and comfortable in multiple settings with a variety of people and other dogs, he will tend to react more calmly and with less aggression.

You must accept that other people out walking their dogs may experience with apprehension at the sight of an animal as large and powerful as a fully-grown American Bulldog.

Truth be told, little dogs are often the instigators of trouble because they have a tendency to bark and growl first, agitating larger dogs. Exercise extreme caution with your pet around smaller animals.

Don't adopt an attitude that yours is the sole right of way. You don't own the street and yours is not the only dog out there on a leash! Do not contribute to potential problems by refusing to change your route. That accomplishes nothing.

Watch what's going on around you and avoid potential trouble. Walk with your head up and scan the surrounding area. If you see another dog owner approaching with a smaller dog on a leash, for instance, cross the street or go down a side street to avoid a confrontation.

Learn to read how well other dog owners are controlling their animals. If you see an approaching walker with a dog straining, pulling at the lead, and barking, this is someone who is not in control of their pet. Get out of their way!

Other bad cues include repeated admonitions like "no" and "get down" or "stop that," which the dog completely ignores. Look for nervous body language in the other owner, and an overall sense that they are the ones being walked rather than the ones in charge of the walk.

If avoidance is impossible and you are constantly encountering smaller dogs or ill-behaved ones on your route, consider muzzling your pet. While this won't stop pulling and growling, it will forestall biting.
Depending on the size of your American Bulldog, a muzzle should not cost more than $30 / £17.5.

Never, under any circumstances, allow your American Bulldog off leash in an area you cannot control. Chance encounters with other dogs and people can go badly wrong with this breed, especially if your pet is startled.

Even an extremely well trained American Bulldog can make a snap decision based on an instinctual response no matter what "command" you are issuing.

You must retain physical control of your dog at all times. Remember, this is a guardian breed. Your dog isn't necessarily being "bad," he thinks he's doing his job.

Learn your dog's likes and dislikes and don't put the animal or yourself in a situation that is ripe for trouble. If the sight of a kid on a skateboard makes your American Bulldog go bonkers, don't walk by the skate park! If the dog has a thing about people in uniforms, steer clear of mailmen, police officers, and UPS drivers!

Ideally you will be able to work with your dog to eliminate or at least moderate these responses, but all dogs are individuals. I had one American Bulldog who was convinced all motorcycles were demons from hell.

If we were in the car on the freeway and a biker passed us, the dog would lose his mind. I was never able to quell this reaction. He hated the sight of a motorcycle until the day of his death.

In all situations in which your dog is likely to exhibit a poor reaction, controlling your own demeanor is essential. I can't tell you how many bad meetings in dog parks I've witnessed that begin with a human panicking before either dog has done a thing.

Of course vigilance and fast interaction are required, but so is calm. Dogs pick up on our emotions. If you are afraid, nervous, and jumpy, your dog will be all that and more because he believes it is his job to protect you. Even when you're just deciding to alter the direction of your walk to avoid trouble, do so *calmly*.

When humans speak loudly, dogs interpret that as "barking" and respond in kind. Also, one dog barking will elicit barking from another. Keeping things low key and quiet sends the critical cue to your dog that everything is fine and you, the alpha, are in complete charge.

If another dog walker is completely oblivious and approaches you anyway, issue a polite and friendly warning. "He doesn't like little dogs" or "I'm sorry, but we need to keep them apart." If the other owner assures you their dog is friendly say nicely, but firmly. "That's great, but my dog isn't friendly."

Sometimes a dog will bristle at the sight of another human for no reason you can immediately understand. Some dogs, for instance, have a thing about people in hats.

I had one dog that would bark and growl at family friends if they had something on their head, and then wag his tail

and go running to them for scratches as soon as the offending hat was taken off.

If you see your dog reacting to someone who clearly is not a threat, keep the dog at a safe distance, but smile and say hello to the person. Don't do anything to validate the dog's suspicious reaction or it will escalate the next time your pet thinks he's seeing the same "monster."

When you are walking an American Bulldog, it is also important not to get "into it" with another dog owner. If you begin to have words with someone, your pet will read your body language and hear the strain and anger in your voice. This will activate his guardian response. He will, in his mind, be rushing to your aid, but in reality he'll just make things worse.

These are the kinds of altercations that wind up with someone getting bitten or being injured seriously. Keep your cool. Your dog is literally depending on it! You are his interpreter in the human world. Always send a calm, in control message.

Chapter 7 – Training Your American Bulldog

Although most aspects of standard obedience training apply to American Bulldogs as they would to any other breed, there are specific concerns with these dogs in the areas of housebreaking, separation anxiety, and aggression.

Housebreaking

American Bulldogs have a reputation for being difficult to housebreak. It may be a full 6 months before your dog gets the hang of things, another reason why using a crate is absolutely essential. Still, be prepared to take your young dog out 8-12 times a day to avoid accidents.

After 6 months, the necessary trips should drop to 6-8 a day, and then 5-7 when the dog is 8 months and older. Adult dogs are taken out approximately four times a day: first thing in the morning, after breakfast, at noon, in the evening around supper, and right before bedtime.

Consistency and patience are required to enforce this routine. If possible, create an area in the backyard, perhaps covered in crushed stone that your dog can come to associate as his "bathroom."

Many dogs have a tactile response to locations where they are allowed to urinate and defecate, so making that spot feel unique is helpful. When the dog is on a surface that doesn't feel right as a place to "go," they typically will wait.

Build trips outside around waking, feeding, and

sleeping.Do not deviate from this routine. You will only confuse your dog and contribute to the frequency of accidents if you take him out at odd times of the day.

Don't punish a dog for having an accident in the house. Clean the spot thoroughly with an enzymatic cleaner to eliminate the odor and return to the dog's normal routine. Nature's Miracle Stain and Odor Removal is an excellent product for these kinds of incidents. A 32-ounce (0.9 liter) bottle sells for $5 (£2.97).

Dealing with Separation Anxiety

Crate training is an essential component in housebreaking an American Bulldog and in dealing with the separation anxiety from which this breed often suffers. In regard to housebreaking, a dog associates the crate as his den and will not soil it.

This same sense, however, also prevents the kind of "acting out" associated with the extreme nervousness of a pack animal left on its own too long. This can translate to destroyed furniture, soiled carpets, and off-the-walls agitation when you come home at the end of the day.

Behavior of this nature does not indicate that you have a bad dog, but rather one that is severely stressed. Instead of trying to correct this problem after its present, your best course of action is to prevent the reaction in the first place.

American Bulldogs are social animals. Being left home alone makes them highly uncomfortable and anxious, but even life events can trigger an episode of separation anxiety. This might include the death of a member of the family or of another pet, alterations in your work routine, or moving to a new house. Changes of this magnitude are often confusing and worrisome to a dog.

For animals that have been adopted from rescue situations, being left alone can force them to relive their sense of abandonment every time you walk out the door. They don't know if you're coming back or if once again they will be left on their own to survive. Just imagine how you would feel under similar circumstances. It must be awful!

In addition to providing your dog with a crate as a safe "den" while you are away, also make sure that your pet is well exercised before you go out. This will help him to sleep while you're away rather than trying to soothe his own anxiety by "self-medicating" with inappropriate behavior.

Dealing with Barking and Aggression

As I have already discussed, American Bulldogs are strongly driven by their instincts, both in the pursuit of prey, but also in the tasks at which they excel, bringing down bulls and other livestock.

Care should be taken with these dogs around many kinds of animals. Never try to keep an American Bulldog with a cat and be extremely cautious with smaller dogs. It is imperative that this breed be taught, from a young age, how to accurately perceive threats based on your cues and responses.

Standard obedience training should begin at less than six months of age, with the dog graduating to work with an experienced instructor once the basic commands are mastered (sit, stay, down, heel, and come).

The goal of training that curbs barking and aggression is to clearly establish your own role as leader of the pack. Additionally, classes with a trainer facilitate socialization around other dogs and people in controlled circumstances. You have as much to learn as the dog!

Being well socialized does not make an American Bulldog a less effective guardian. It does, however, make him an effective judge of the people he encounters in relation to pack and territory status.

The more deeply you are bonded with your dog, the more correctly he will be able to read your mood and attitude.

Play at least 3 times a day with your puppy. American Bulldogs play rough! Don't allow your young dog to bite. If your pet's teeth touch your skin, immediately grab the dog's snout and say sternly, "No biting." Offer the dog a suitable toy as an alternative.

If the dog will not settle down, place the puppy on its back and hold it there for as long as it takes for the animal to get still. Then and only then offer your pet a toy. If this doesn't work, immediately crate the puppy.

> **Tip:** Consistency is key in training an American Bulldog. Do not let them get away with poor behavior even once. A breed this dominant is perfectly capable of taking advantage of a weak willed master.

Use the exact same protocol for growling and barking. All play must be on your terms and the puppy must know from the beginning that you are in charge. Do not engage in games like "tug of war" that encourage aggression.

Instead, employ games of fetch with balls and other toys, or throw a Frisbee to encourage your pet's ability to execute stunning athletic jumps. You can facilitate a great deal of fun, bonding activity with an American Bulldog while still keeping the interaction low key and non-threatening.

Socialization

While your American Bulldog is young, take the dog with you into acceptable venues where you can mold and direct its behavior around strangers and other dogs in a positive way. Big box pet stores that allow animals are a good option, as are restaurants with patios that are pet friendly.

If you have children, or if there are children living nearby, ask their parents for permission to allow supervised playtime to let the puppy get used to kids.

This is extremely important, since many tragic incidents with guardian breeds occur when dogs are not socialized to behave well around the very young *and* the very old.

The point of socialization is to create awareness in your American Bulldog of the distinction between "good" and "bad" people. It will also teach your dog to look to you for guidance in reading a new situation.

Dog parks are not the best place to allow your American Bulldog pup to interact with other dogs. Instead, look for supervised "doggy daycare" situations and group classes.

You cannot count on the behavior of other dogs in parks, nor will you have the advantage of expert advice and assistance.

Invest in Professional Assistance

In the vast majority of cases, humans need far more training than their dogs. Experts are in agreement that many companion animals that act out do so because they are behaving as the alpha in the home "pack."

Again – and yes, I know I am repeating myself -- American

Bulldogs are dominant by nature, so you cannot be a wishy-washy human around them!

With this breed, you must be the boss. Period. This doesn't mean being unduly harsh or authoritarian, however. It does mean being calm, confident, and quietly in charge of all interactions and reactions.

Dogs feel safe when they know they are being protected and "advised" by their leader. That should and must be you.

It's one thing to let a Bichon Frise or a Chihuahua run roughshod over your life. You can pick up either and be done with any confrontation. American Bulldogs are large, highly assertive animals quite capable of wrestling livestock to the ground.

Do not make the mistake of thinking you can physically stop your dog from doing anything when he becomes truly enraged or thinks it is necessary to protect you from a perceived danger.

> **Tip:** Obedience training is a proactive approach to avoid trouble, not a desperate attempt to correct problem behavior once it is already established!

Investing in professional training for your American Bulldog is like buying an insurance policy against aggression and misbehavior. And actually, going to a class with your dog can be a lot of fun. You'll learn a lot about how dogs think and interact.

But the real point – again – it to be a proactive American Bulldog owner. Don't let problems get started in the first place! This is truly a breed that is as good or as bad as its master.

You have to be ready to commit to this dog every bit as much as you expect him to commit to you.

Never for one minute lose site of the responsibility you are assuming in crafting and ensuring appropriate responses and good behavior from your American Bulldog.

Chapter 8 – Diet and Nutrition

As they age, dogs will do best on a graduated program of nutrition targeted for the distinct phases of their lives. Puppies are voracious eaters, consuming about twice as much as their adult counterparts until they reach 4 months of age.

On average, a puppy of less than 4 months should be fed 3-4 cups (709-946 grams) of food per day divided into four meals. At 4-6 months that can be decreased to 2.75 to 3 cups (650-709 grams) a day spread out over three feedings.

> **Tip:** Don't leave food out for your American Bulldog, a practice known as "free feeding." Feed him measured amounts at set times.
>
> These dogs are very bad to wolf down their food, eat too much, and even develop obsessive reactions to their food bowls, which can be a driver for aggressive behavior.

After age six-months, your American Bulldog can receive an adult ration of 1.5 to 2 cups (354-473 grams) of food per day in two meals.

Do not free feed with this breed since they have a tendency to eat too fast and gorge themselves. Obesity is a major problem with American Bulldogs and can contribute to joint disorders including hip and elbow dysplasia.

Use a regular feeding schedule and set portions of food with only very limited treats.

Picking Dog Food

With so many brands of dog food on the market, making a precise recommendation is difficult. Clearly you should opt for the highest quality premium dry food you can afford.

In the beginning, give your puppy whatever it's used to eating at the kennel. Suddenly switching to a new food will only cause gastrointestinal upsets.

With any food, read the label to ensure the first ingredients are meat, fishmeal, or whole grains. Avoid products with a lot of meat by-products or cornmeal.

These are fillers with very little nutritional value that do only increase the dog's output of solid waste.

Since portion control is important with this breed and wet foods are more difficult to measure, your American Bulldog should be fine with good quality dry food and plenty of clean, cool water.

Specific Recommendations

American Bulldogs are very hard working even if they are just going about the business of being family companions. They are real powerhouses of energy and they need good fuel to maintain their usual pace.

To this end, there are some specific recommendations relative to very high-quality foods formulated for more athletic dogs.

- Crude protein should be no less than 30 percent.
- Crude fat should be no less than 20 percent.
- Fiber content should be 4 percent or less.

Within those parameters, many American Bulldog enthusiasts recommend the following foods. All are, arguably, quite expensive, but they do offer an exceptional level of nutrition.

- **Orijen**, which offers a range of free-run poultry, wild-caught fish, and free-range red meat diets. Approximately $75 / £44 per 30 lbs. / 13.6 kg.

- **Eagle Pack**, which is the official dog food of the Iditarod sled dog race. Specifically consider the Power Adult dog food. Approximately $45 / £26 per 30 lbs. / 13.6 kg.

- **Diamond Pet Food**, which has a good level of protein and fats for working dogs at a more affordable price point. Approximately $45 / £26 per 40 lbs. / 18.14 kg.

Although it is difficult to precisely calculate how long a bag of food will last, let's use Orijen as an example. One cup of dry adult food from this brand weighs .25 lbs. / 0.11 kg.

So, at 4 cups per pound (0.45 kg) a 29.7 lb. (13.47 kg) bag (which I rounded up to 30 lbs. / 13.6 kg above) would yield 118 cups and therefore would last about 2 months.

Clearly if you have a larger American Bulldog that needs an extra cup per day, you might get only a month to six weeks out of one bag.

Avoid Human Foods

It's always tempting to give a dog a bite of something off the table. Don't let this behavior get started! Again, think about the potential for aggression with this breed.

The last thing you want is to be out in public with your American Bulldog and have him suddenly decide that a child's ice cream cone is "his."

Use only commercial dog treats and never let "snacks" account for more than 5% of your pet's dietary intake per day.

It's a good idea to limit treats to rewards for good behavior to create a powerful association in your dog's mind that doing "right" things gets him "good stuff."

Many "people" foods are very bad for dogs and even potentially fatal. Items you definitely do NOT want to give your dog include:

- Raw fish, pork, or chicken
- Alcohol
- Chocolate
- Raisins
- Mushrooms
- Onions and garlic
- Walnuts or macadamia nuts
- Human vitamins (especially those with iron)

Although dogs do love bones, the danger of lacerations from splintering is quite high. It's far safer to use commercial chew toys.

Clearly this is not a comprehensive list. There are many other human foods dogs should not have, so take the much easier route. Don't let him eat human food at all!

Chapter 9 – American Bulldog Health

Finding a qualified veterinarian and cultivating a solid working relationship with that person lays the foundation for a lifetime of solid healthcare for your American Bulldog.

If you do not already have a vet, ask the breeder for a recommendation in your area or plan on interviewing multiple doctors until you find one that has experience with this breed.

Visit each clinic in advance of actually going in with your dog. Be clear that you are making the appointment to explore working with the doctor. Pay for the visit.

Vets are busy people. Don't waste anyone's time. Go in with your questions already prepared. These should include such things as:

- How long has this practice been open?

- What are your hours?

- What provisions do you make for after hours emergency care?

- What specific procedures can be performed in the office and what would require consultation with a specialist?

- Do you also offer boarding and grooming services? If not, do you recommend facilities that do?
- Have you treated American Bulldogs before? Are you treating any dogs now?

- How many vets are on staff here?

Ask for a schedule of fees for normal care and procedures. Pay close attention to how your questions are answered. Do you like the manner of the staff? Does the clinic seem efficient? clean? well kept?

Look around the waiting area. Do you see a bulletin board with thank you notes and pictures of patients? If so, you can be confident you are working with a practice in which the staff is friendly, open, and fosters a sense of connection with the clientele.

Also take note of the equipment. Does it seem modern? Are the doctor's diplomas and credentials displayed prominently? Ask if the vet(s) engage in continuing education and if so, how often?

The First Vet Visit

Provided you like what you see and hear at one of the clinics, schedule a visit to go in with your American Bulldog puppy. Take all pertinent medical records and plan on discussing vaccinations and having the dog spayed or neutered.

Expect a routine examination to evaluate the dog's current condition, which will include checking heart and lung function. Baseline measurements and current weight will be recorded to judge your pet's growth rate in the coming months.

Vaccinations

Puppies usually receive their first shots when they are 6-7 weeks old. The first vaccination is a combination to provide protection against distemper, hepatitis, parvovirus, parainfluenza and coronavirus.

Booster shots are then given at 9, 12, and 16 weeks. In some areas, the vaccine for Lyme disease is started at 16 weeks and boosted at 18 weeks.

The rabies vaccination is given at 12-16 weeks of age and then annually for life.

Deworming

Typically vets ask owners to collect a stool sample before a puppy's fist exam so a precautionary test for worms can be run. When you purchase your pet from a breeder, it is unlikely that the dog will have intestinal parasites, but it is certainly not out of the realm of possibility.

Worm infestations are easily addressed with an initial course of a deworming agent followed by repeat treatment in 10 days to get any remaining eggs.

Roundworms are the most likely culprits, with the only evidence being tiny white granules around the anus. Other external parasites must be detected through microscopic examination. Tapeworms, if present, can be life threatening and require veterinary treatment.

Spaying and Neutering

Typically the adoption contract for a pet quality American Bulldog requires that the animal be spayed or neutered before it reaches six months of age.

The provision is inserted to protect the kennel's bloodlines and to stem the tide of unwanted companion animals.

With this breed, however, there are both medical and behavioral benefits to the surgery. Both males and females will have a decreased risk of developing a number of cancers associated with the reproductive organs.

Neutering males, however, carries the added plus of markedly reducing aggressive behavior and curbing some of the breed's highly territorial instincts. It is a myth, however, to think that neutering a male will render him useless as a guard dog.

To the contrary, the surgery will make the animal much more controllable, and therefore much more trainable so that it will function as an *effective* guard dog.

Be on the Alert for Signs of Illness

Beyond these initial, routine procedures that start your dog's long-term healthcare, discuss with your vet the things you should watch out for as ongoing preventive healthcare.

Since you will be living with and interacting with the dog on a daily basis, you are in the best position to detect even the subtle changes in mood and behavior that could indicate the onset of a health problem. If you are troubled in any way about your pet's overall wellbeing, even if you can't quite put your finger on what's wrong, go to the vet!

Obviously with any potential illness, the sooner it is detected and treated; the better. Some general signs that may be cause for concern include the following considerations.

Coughing or Wheezing

While it is not unusual for any animal to cough, you should be aware of how any persistent cough sounds and how it presents in relation to your dog's overall behavior and appetite. Coughing can indicate numerous conditions:

- kennel cough
- heartworm
- cardiac disease
- bacterial infections
- parasites
- tumors
- allergies

If your American Bulldog has a case of kennel cough, he will have a dry, hacking cough. This is often the result of being boarded in a poorly ventilated, overly warm area in close proximity to other dogs.

In the vast majority of cases, kennel cough, which is really canine bronchitis, resolves, but your dog may need to see the vet to get a cough suppressant to ease the symptoms. The vet may also suggest the use of a humidifier to soothe your pet's irritated airways.

If, however, the dog seems to be coughing for no apparent reason, the vet will want to order blood work and X-rays and to test for heartworms. When fluid is present on the lungs, a sample will be drawn to check for infection. This is often the case if, in addition to the coughing, the animal's breathing is labored and there is significant wheezing.

Do not be concerned about seeming like an overly protective "parent." If the coughing is a consequence of heartworms, immediate treatment is essential.

Heartworms

Heartworms are very easy to detect, but difficult and expensive to cure, so your best course of action is *always* preventive measures.

The worms, *Dirofilaria Immitis,* enter the system through a mosquito bite. They are long, thin parasites that invade the cardiac muscle, blocking blood vessels and causing bleeding, which, typically, leads to heart failure and death.

Symptoms include coughing, fainting, and an intolerance to exercise. At your puppy's first visit to the vet, discuss heartworm prevention, decide on the best course of action, and stick with the program!

Bad Breath

At one time or another, we've all been blasted in the face with doggy bad breath. American Bulldogs, like any other breed, can suffer from halitosis.

Understand that this is a symptom, not a condition. It points to dental issues like plaque buildup or even periodontal disease.

Regular dental exams at the vet's should be an aspect of

routine health care, but you should also accustom your pet at an early age to having his teeth cleaned at home with canine specific toothpaste and some type of brush.

Although there are actual dog toothbrushes, I prefer the "finger brushes" that fit on your finger like a cap. It's much easier to achieve good coverage on the teeth via this method, and to spread the toothpaste all around the mouth.

These items and appropriate dental chews are available in your vet's office. If you are unsure how to use them, or the correct way to train your puppy to tolerate this procedure ask the vet and/or your dog trainer for help.

American Bulldogs connect so strongly with their owners that if you start dental care when they are puppies, they typically do not object. This is not an area of healthcare for your pet that you can afford to let slide. Other problems that can cause bad breath include:

- sinus infections
- canine diabetes
- tonsillitis
- respiratory disease
- kidney disease
- liver disease
- gastrointestinal blockages
- cancer

For this reason, do not ignore instances of halitosis. Always have bad breath evaluated by your vet.

Other Potential Warning Signs

There is no substitute for an intimate knowledge of a dog as an individual. Always trust your instinct where your pet is concerned. However, any of the following may warrant a trip to the vet.

- drooling for no apparent reason
- increased water consumption
- increased urination
- any change in appetite
- weight changes (gain or loss)
- any change in activity
- disinterest / depression
- difficulty moving, especially climbing stairs
- sleeping more than usual
- shaking or slinging of the head

- any growth or sore
- eyes that do not appear normal (dry, red, running, cloudy)

Always trust your own instincts and your one-on-one understanding of your pet. Never hesitate to consult with your vet.

Conditions Common in American Bulldogs

With an average lifespan of 10-15 years, American Bulldogs are physically active, strong, healthy dogs. Typically health issues are found within given genetic lines rather than being universally present across the breed.

The conditions that do appear in the general American Bulldog population include:

- neuronal ceroid lipofuscinosis (NCL)
- Ichthyosis
- kidney and thyroid disorders
- ACL tears
- hip and elbow dysplasia
- entropion and ectropion
- deafness
- bone cancer

There is also a predisposition for this breed to be prone to allergies, typically indicated by rashes and a runny nose. Most can be easily managed with doses of Benadryl.

Neuronal Ceroid Lipofuscinosis

Neuronal Ceroid Lipofuscinosis is not simple to explain. Essentially we are talking about a "lysosomal storage disorder." For most of us, that means nothing, so let's come at it a different way. Lysosomes are structures in cells. They are there to break down waste products generated by the cell.

If a dog has neuronal ceroid lipofuscinosis, he doesn't have an enzyme necessary to break down specific types of fat or protein in the cells.

This causes a lot of debris to build up in all kinds of cells in the body, but particularly in the cells of the nervous system, the neurons. The result is a breakdown in the dog's ability to function mentally and muscularly.

When the condition is present, the dog will seem perfectly normal, but as early as 6 months or as late as 4-6 years of age, symptoms will manifest, with a progressive loss of abilities. (NCL doesn't just happen in dogs, by the way. It can also be present in humans.)

You may start to see mental confusion and an inability to problem solve. The dog may seem to be losing coordination and balance. This will lead to a strange gait and ultimately seizures. As the disease progresses the animal experiences:

- visual disturbances leading to blindness
- behavioral changes including aggressiveness
- dementia

- aimless wandering
- depression

There is no cure for NCL, but the rate of progression varies greatly by individual and by the specific type of NCL present. All are ultimately fatal. Currently there are 7 identified variation of the disease in dogs.

NCL has been conclusively linked to recessively inherited genes in the following breeds:

- American Bulldog
- American Staffordshire Terrier
- Australian Cattle Dogs
- Australian Shepherd
- Border Collie
- Chihuahua
- Cocker Spaniel
- Dachshund
- Dalmatian
- English Setter
- Golden Retriever
- Japanese Retriever
- Labrador Retriever
- Miniature Schnauzer
- Pit Bull Terriers
- Polish Lowland Sheepdog
- Salukis
- Tibetan Terrier

- Welch Corgi

The insidious problem with a genetic disorder like NCL is that the recessive genes may pass through several generations without actually affecting individual animals.

Two carriers must breed for the NCL gene to become active. If this occurs, 25% of the pups will have NCL and at least two-thirds will be carriers.

Only molecular diagnostic testing can determine if any dog is at risk for developing NCL. Do not accept any other assurance of the absence of this problem in a line of American Bulldogs and insist on seeing official documentation proving that the test has been performed.

Ichthyosis

The genetic skin disorder ichthyosis, which can also affect humans, is not fatal, but it does cause the dog life-long discomfort. The first signs that the disease is present typically occur around 2 weeks of age.

The puppies will have flaky, wrinkled skin that makes them appear dirty in comparison to their littermates.

Typically the condition worsens with age. Heavily affected animals require daily bathing and the application of oil to combat the accompanying severe itching. If the skin becomes damaged from constant scratching and chewing, the window is opened for serious infection.

Most vets actually do not recognize ichthyosis and will treat the lesions as bacterial or fungal infections. The treatment may lead to short-term improvements, but there is no actual cure for the disease; it can only be managed with palliative care.

The condition is passed on via a dominant-recessive inheritance with three possible genotypes:

- Ichthyosis clear (0/0), the individual has two intact genes and can only pass those onto offspring. No offspring will be affected so long as one parent is ichthyosis clear.

- Ichthyosis carrier (0/+), the individual has one intact and one defective gene. The individual is a healthy carrier with a 50/50 chance of passing on one of the other genes to offspring.

- Ichthyosis affected (+/+), the individual is affected and has two defective genes. If bred, the defective gene will be passed on.

If an ichthyosis clear dog is bred to a carrier, half of the litter will be clear and half will be carriers. Dogs that are carriers are healthy, and can't be recognized on sight. If two carriers are bred, a quarter of the offspring will have ichthyosis, a quarter will be clear, and half will be carriers.

There has been a specific gene-test for ichthyosis in American Bulldogs since 2011 that can identify every genotype and completely avoid the mating of two carriers.

Verify with the breeder that this test has been performed on the puppy's parents.

ACL Tears

Like all active breeds, American Bulldogs can suffer from a torn cranial cruciate ligament. A dog's knee is not so different from our own, and this injury is similar to a torn ACL in a human.

If you are with your dog when the injury occurs, you may hear the ligament pop. The dog will immediately begin to limp or carry the leg because the injury is initially painful. If there is no accompanying arthritis and the cartilage is not torn, the pain will subside. Surgery may not be required, but in either case, your pet will enjoy a complete recoveryin about 90 percent of cases. In large breeds like the American Bulldog, however, surgery is recommended, as is a course of pain medication and anti-inflammatory drugs.

The procedure serves to stabilize the joint, but requires a 1-3 month recovery during which extensive activity must be avoided. During this period, passive exercises like swimming can help to burn off excess energy while restoring strength and range of motion.

Hip and Elbow Dysplasia

Many heavy breeds including the American Bulldog suffer from hip and elbow dysplasia. The condition is caused by a genetic malformation of the ball and socket joints in both locations or by an injury.

The dysplasia may take one of two forms. Either the fit of the joint is too tight so that motion is restricted, or due to chronic looseness, the dog suffers from repetitive dislocations.

Either variation can range in intensity from a mildly annoying problem that flares up intermittently to a severely debilitating condition accompanied by pain and inflammation.

The first indication that something is wrong is typically a sort of hopping, abnormal gait or limp. It can appear in dogs as young as four months or at any stage of life.

Often treatment requires little more than pain medication

and anti-inflammatory drugs, but in severe cases, surgery may be indicated, especially if a secondary case of arthritis begins to manifest.

Entropion and Ectropion

American Bulldogs sometimes suffer from abnormal eyelids, conditions called entropion and ectropion depending on the direction the eyelid turns.

If it turns inward, irritating the cornea, the issue is "entropion." Dogs with one or more of the eyelids turned outward (usually the lower) suffer from "ectropion."

Either condition becomes apparent in puppies within the first few weeks after birth. They will squint, suffer excessive tearing, or, in instances of extropion, the red tissue around the eye (conjunctiva) is visible and subject to irritation and infection.

In most cases both entropion and ectropion resolve as the dog grows, but in severe cases a canine ophthalmologist must intervene to tack the lids with stitches that remain in place for a period of days or even weeks.

Sometimes the procedure must be performed a second time before the correct "fit" is achieved. During healing, artificial tears must be put in the dog's eyes to prevent drying. Without this intervention, however, the puppy's eyesight can be compromised or lost.

Congenital Deafness

There are approximately 85 breeds, including American Bulldogs, in which congenital deafness surfaces. The issue can be linked to multiple causes including a genetic defect, but also to:

- intrauterine infections
- ototoxic drugs (gentamicin)
- liver disorders
- toxic exposures (before or after birth)

Pinning down the exact cause for the deafness is often impossible. Dogs with white pigmentation are especially susceptible.

Typically hearing loss progresses to total deafness during the first weeks of life and is associated with degeneration of the flow of blood to the cochlea causing cell death.

This process seems to be associated with the absence of pigment-producing melanocytes in the blood vessels, which are thought to play a role in maintaining cochlear potassium levels.

In some breeds, like the Doberman pinscher, congenital deafness is often complicated by vestibular irregularities that destroy the dog's balance.

This is caused by a slightly different version of the issue that leads to the death of the small hairs in the ear that effect equilibrium

Bone Cancer

American Bulldogs are also one of the breeds that are susceptible to the development of bone cancer. Osteosarcoma (OSA) is the most common bone tumor in dogs, accounting for about 85% of skeletal cancer.

The tumor is most often associated with the "wrist" on the front leg with growths on the back legs less common.

The cancer can appear on any bone, however, and typically appears in middle-aged to older American Bulldogs. The exact cause of the prevalence of bone cancer in the breed is not known.

In about 95% of cases the cancer will spread to the organs and may already have done so by the time the illness is detected. The standard treatment is amputation of the affected limb with chemotherapy to treat cancer elsewhere in the body.

About half of the dogs diagnosed with bone cancer undergo amputation and treatment are alive one year later. Twenty-five percent survive two years.

On average, however, the surgery and treatment will only extend the animal's life about six months. It is only in very rare cases that bone cancer can be cured.

The cause of death is almost always the spread of the cancer to the vital organs. American Bulldogs are so agile and athletic, they adapt incredibly well to the amputation and can have an extremely high quality of life for whatever time they do have left.

Chapter 10 – As Your American Bulldog Ages

The lifespan of the American Bulldog is 10-15 years, so by the time your pet is 7 or 8, he qualifies as a "senior citizen." The standard rule is that the larger the dog, the shorter his projected lifespan, but that varies greatly by individual.

Normal Signs of Aging

Our dogs are very much like us as they approach the sunset of their lives. I have often caught myself calling an aging pet "Little Old Man" or "Little Old Lady" because that's exactly what they are!

Some of the things you will typically see in elderly pets include:

Gray Hair

One of the most obvious changes you will see as your dog ages is the same thing that happens to us. His hair will begin to gray, first on the muzzle and face and then around the eyes.

Don't worry about the silver coming into his coat, however. Dogs wear the look well, simply appearing to be the wise creatures we already know they are.

Changes in Activity Levels

Your pet's activity level will drop and he'll be much more content to nap and less inclined toward raucous play and long, exhausting walks. Oddly enough, however, in American Bulldogs this may simply mean your pet drops down to a "normal" level of activity. You'll likely just notice that he's not wearing *you* out any more.

You may see either weight loss or gain, and if joint dysfunction and arthritis are present, the dog may limp, have trouble getting up, or be reluctant to climb stairs. If the animal is in pain, he could nip or act aggressive if touched or bothered.

Pain in the joints, especially in the hindquarters could affect the dog's ability to maintain his usual bathroom habits, or to go without soiling himself.

Diminished Senses and Cognitive Changes

His coat may become thinner and less glossy, and skin growths including benign fatty lipomas typically appear. It's usual to see a diminishment of sight and hearing. His breath may be bad due to tooth decay.

Older American Bulldogs tend to be more likely to experience separation anxiety. They know their abilities are no longer sharp and they are not as effective as guardians. This makes them nervous, and they need the security of having their pack leader – you – nearby to protect them.

Many old dogs experience canine cognitive dysfunction or "old-dog" syndrome, which is the canine version of dementia. The animal will forget his daily routine, show signs of confusion, become lethargic and disinterested, and fail to recognize you.

> **Tip:** Continue to play with your American Bulldog throughout his life, challenging him intellectually to help stave off the potential that as he gets older he will develop "doggy dementia."

There is good evidence that suggests, however, that continuing to play and challenge your pet with games – even those that are less physically demanding – will keep the dog interested and more mentally alert as he ages. This is basically the "use it or lose it" theory.

American Bulldogs with hormonal fluctuations due to diabetes or thyroid disease experience increased hunger so they become aggressive about guarding their food to the point of obsession.

Expect Increased Vet Visits

To understand all the changes your pet is undergoing, be sure to go in for annual vet visits, and to increase those trips as needed for blood work, dental cleanings, and other procedures to make your pet more comfortable as his body is changing.It is imperative that any new problems or diseases be diagnosed and treated as soon as possible.

It is not uncommon for an individual dog to be alert, hardy, in great shape, and then to suddenly fall into a decline and pass suddenly. This is a heartbreaking shift for the humans, but in a way this kind of end is a blessing for your pet. The dog remains "himself" to the end, enjoying his life to the very last moment.

Let your veterinarian guide you in what tests should be performed like:

- EKG to judge coronary function
- blood pressure tests
- lab tests for thyroid function
- vision tests for glaucoma
- chest x-rays
- screening for tumors
- fecal samples for parasites and other digestive issues

Modifications in diet will likely be required. At the very least the dog will need a senior formula food, but often older dogs must be put on specific prescription diets with lower fat or protein content relative to a diagnosed medical condition.

You do not want to allow an older dog to become too thin, but neither should he be allowed to pack on the pounds as his metabolism slows down.

Obesity is risky for older dogs because it creates an open window for heart disease and it worsens the effects of joint dysfunction and arthritis on mobility and quality of life.

Managing the Dog's Environment

Regardless of what your dog is going through physically and temperamentally, he is still the pet you've known and loved. As he ages, he simply needs extra attention and a different level of care and patience. Help your aging American Bulldog by keeping his environment consistent, especially if he is experiencing loss of vision.

Older dogs with cognitive dysfunction depend on their daily routine. Sometimes muscle memory takes over and the dog just goes through the motions of a "normal" day. This is a good thing even if your pet is "out of it" because lapsing into automatic routine will also keep him eating longer.

Older dogs are less tolerant of heat and cold, so make certain your pet is warm in the winter and cool in the summer. Do not allow him to become chilled or overheated. If necessary, buy sweaters or coats for cold weather.

Euthanasia

There is perhaps no more difficult topic to address than considering an end of life decision for a beloved pet. I have a very strong feeling that no one should ever tell you what to do in this regard. Your veterinarian is, of course, your wisest counsel, but I have a firm belief that in the end, your pet will tell you when the time has come.

On many occasions I have had to make this choice and I can say with complete confidence that each dog I have helped to transition has gone in peace and free of pain. I have always been very lucky to have the help of outstanding veterinary professionals for whom I have the highest regard.

My vets have not only known my animals and been able to truly judge their physical and emotional condition, but these same doctors know me. I have one criterion in all my decisions. Is there anything that can be done to help this dog and to keep him happy, healthy, and enjoying his life?

If the answer is yes, we're not "done." If the answer is no, and the dog is clearly unhappy and suffering, then the decision, though painful is much clearer.

I have seen dogs survive amputations and chemotherapy and go on living as their usual joyful selves for months with cancer in their bodies. I have no right for my own convenience to take the life of a dog who is pain free and still living.

Now, understand, that is my ethic. I am lucky. I have never been driven by finances to make an end of life decision for my pet. No one. Absolutely no one can judge you for the choices you make.

So long as you are at peace in your heart that your beloved companion has been treated with love and respect, and that you have done the best you can possibly do for a creature that is your friend and family member that is more than "good enough." It is everything.

The final injection itself is quick and pain free. Typically vets are quite willing to come to your home or to go anywhere else that gives you and your animal comfort, like a favorite spot in the park. I do counsel picking someplace private and making sure there is nothing to frighten or startle your dog.

Afterwards, give yourself all the time you need to grieve your loss. People who do not have pets do not fully understand the bond that forms between human and animal. The ties that grow over time with an American Bulldog are extremely strong. They are one of the most loyal breeds I have ever encountered.

I cannot tell you that there will not be a hole in your heart. There will. But you will also be filled with memories of the time you were allowed to spend with a truly exceptional creature.
Know that to release the suffering of an animal in a humane

way is a great act of kindness and the ultimate expression of the responsibility we assume the day we adopt them as puppies.

Pet Insurance to Defray Healthcare Costs

Given the impressive advancements in veterinary medicine over the past 25 years, there are now real and viable treatments to effectively cure disease and to maintain a companion animal's life over the long term.

Consequently, the projected life expectancy for many breeds has actually increased, which is great news for dedicated animal lovers!

Once these factors are taken into consideration, pet insurance to defray veterinary expenses can be an excellent decision for you and your American Bulldog.

In some cases you can take out a comprehensive policy providing coverage for accidents, illness, and even some hereditary and chronic conditions for only $25 / £16.25 per month.

(Obviously benefit levels and deductibles vary by company and breed. Most insurance underwriters do ask breed specific questions.)

The real benefit to this approach to long-term pet care, as with any insurance policy, is to provide financial assistance for medical emergencies and to create access options for extensive treatment for serious illness.

Paying a small premium per month could allow you the flexibility to opt for a treatment regimen for your pet that you might otherwise be unable to afford, therefore cutting short your time with your dog and forcing an end of life decision before either of you are ready.

To obtain rate quotes and to learn more about details of specific coverage, the companies in the United States and the United Kingdom that are listed below all write health policies for companion animals.

These products are steadily growing in sophistication and offer a reasonable amount of room for premium and benefit negotiation.

United States

24PetWatch
24PetWatch.com

The ASPCA
ASPCAPetInsurance.com

Embrace
EmbracePetInsurance.com

Healthy Paws
HealthyPawsPetInsurance.com

Pets Best
PetsBest.com

Pet First
PetFirst.com

PetInsurance
PetInsurance.com

Pet Premium
Enroll.PetPremium.com

United Kingdom

Animal Friends
Animalfriends.org.uk

Churchill
Churchill.com/pet-insurance

DirectLine
Directline.com/pet-insurance

Healthy Pets
Healthy-pets.co.uk

PetPlan
Petplan.co.uk

VetsMediCover
Vetsmedicover.co.uk

Afterword

If I have done nothing else, I hope I have succeeded in illustrating the uniqueness of the American Bulldog as an agile, athletic guardian with the potential to be a superb family dog and companion.

This is a breed that is incredibly dependent upon a strong relationship with its master to function well in the world. Bred to hunt wild hogs and to bring down large animals like bulls, the American Bulldog cannot help what his genetics and instincts have made of him.

He does, however, have the advantage of a sharp intelligence and an extremely loyal imperative to please and obey his pack leader. That must be you. If you help an American Bulldog to understand what is required of him to be a good dog, he will excel and be an excellent dog.

Part of this formula lies in simply not allowing the dog to be placed in situations where he believes aggression is the correct response.

- If you isolate an American Bulldog and never expose him to the company of others, can you blame him that he regards all strangers as threats?

- If you do not allow him to associate with other dogs, can you blame him if he sees all others of his kind as potential enemies?

- If you allow his prey drive to go unchecked can you

blame him for seeing smaller animals as something to be hunted?

The point I am attempting to make is that in adopting an American Bulldog you are assuming the responsibility to guide and shape the behavior and interactions of a large and powerful dog.

If you have no sense of just how big a 150 lb. / 68 kg dog really is, go on YouTube and watch any one of the many videos of trainers working with this breed. Look at the American Bulldog's massive chest and broad head. Think seriously about the impression he conveys.

Can you see how he might be confused with a Pit Bull or how someone who has a fear of dogs would find him potentially dangerous?

If you adopt this breed, it's your job to manage your dog's place in the world. To run interference for him with those individuals and groups that might choose to label him a "bad dog" on sight with no thought to his individual behavior or history.

When I say this is not a breed for a beginning dog owner, I am quite serious. No pet should be adopted without a real understanding of the animal's physical and emotional needs. The American Bulldog, however, requires significant behavioral insight on the part of his master.

I do not mean to sound as if I am running down this breed. They are absolutely outstanding dogs and I have seen them function as terrific family dogs. I do, however, mean to sound a precautionary note on behalf of the American Bulldog. When you adopt one of these dogs, you are bringing an intelligent living creature into your life who will depend on your entirely.

If you do right by your American Bulldog, he will do right by you. If you can't be what this dog needs, admire him from afar and select a dog that does fit your lifestyle and experience level.

Appendix 1 - Breed Standard

Note: The following breed standard has been reproduced verbatim for reference purposes and to increase your understanding of what is regarded as a "perfect" example of this breed. The only changes that have been made are the addition of some paragraph breaks to facilitate readability in this form.

Source: American Bulldog Association at www.american-bulldog.com/Conformation.html

Revised 2003

Background: The American Bulldog originated as a catch dog (mostly cattle) and property protection dog, in America's Southeast. He was not bred to put on threat displays or to look a certain way.

But, he did need the right equipment to take care of his real bulldog duties, which were confrontational personal and property protection and as a catch dog. He needed to be strong enough to put unruly bulls on the ground and athletic enough to catch hogs that were allowed to free range in a semi-wild state.

General Appearance: The American Bulldog should generate the impression of great strength, agility, endurance and exhibit a well-knit, sturdy, compact frame with the absence of excessive bulk. Males are characteristically larger, heavier boned and more masculine than the bitches.

The AB is a white or white and patched (brindle or red) dog. When patched he can range from the traditional pied markings of a patch over one or both eyes or ears, or a patch on the base of the tail, to a large saddle patch and various other patches.

For judging purposes, distinctions between an ideal "Classic-type" and an ideal "Standard-type" are defined in brackets and in bold.

Size: General: Males - 23 to 27 inches at the withers and weigh from 75 to 120 lbs. Females - 21 to 25 inches at the withers, 60 to 90 lbs. The weight should be proportional to size.

[Classic-type: an ideal male should be 22 to 26 inches at the withers and weigh from 80 to 120 lbs. Females 20 to 24 inches, 60 to 90 lbs.]

[Standard-type: an ideal male should be 23 to 27 inches at the withers and/ weigh from 75 to 110 lbs., females, 21 to 25 inches, 60 to 85 lbs. The weight should be proportional to size.]

Head: Medium in length and broad across skull with pronounced muscular cheeks.

Eyes: Medium in size. Any color. The haw should not be visible. Black eye rims preferred on white dogs. Pink eye rims to be considered a cosmetic fault.

Muzzle: Medium length (2 to 4 in.), square and broad with a strong underjaw. Lips should be full but not pendulous - 42 to 44 teeth.

Classic-type: definite undershot, 1/8 to 1/4 inch preferred. Scissors or even bite is a disqualification. Structural faults are a muzzle under 2 inches or over 4 inches.]

[Standard-type: tight undershot (reverse scissors) preferred. Scissors and even bites are considered a cosmetic fault. Structural faults are a muzzle under 2 inches or longer than 4 inches, pendulous lips, less than 42 teeth, more than 1/4 inch undershot, small teeth or uneven incisors.]

Nose color: Black or grizzle. On black nosed dogs the lips should be black with some pink allowed. A pink nose is considered a cosmetic fault.

Ears: Cropped or uncropped - uncropped preferred.

Neck: Muscular, medium in length, slightly arched, tapering from shoulders to head, with a slight dewlap allowed.

Shoulders: Very muscular with wide sloping blades, shoulders set so elbows are not angled out.

Chest, Back and Loin: The chest should be deep and moderately wide without being excessively wide as to throw the shoulders out. The back should be of medium length, strong and broad.

Loins should be slightly tucked which corresponds to a

slight roach in the back which slopes to the stern. Faults: sway back, narrow or shallow chest, lack of tuck up.

Hindquarters: Very broad and well-muscled and in proportion to the shoulders. Narrow hips are a very serious fault.

Legs: Strong and straight with heavy bone. Front legs should not set too close together or too far apart. Faults: in at the elbows or excessively bowlegged. Rear legs should have a visible angulation of the stifle joint.

Movement: The gait is balanced and smooth, powerful and unhindered suggesting agility with easy, ground covering strides, showing strong driving action in the hind quarters with corresponding reach in front.

As speed increases the feet move toward the center line of the body to maintain balance. Ideally the dog should single-track. The top line remains firm and level, parallel to the line of motion. Head and tail carriage should reflect that of a proud, confident and alert animal.

Movement faults: Any suggestion of clumsiness, tossing and/or rolling of the body, crossing or interference of front or rear legs, short or stilted steps, twisting joints, pacing, paddling, or weaving. Similar movement faults are to be penalized according to the degree to which they interfere with the ability of the dog to work.

Feet: Of moderate size, toes of medium length, well arched and close together, not splayed. Pasterns should be strong, straight and upright.

Tail: Set low, thick at the root, tapering to a point. Tail should not curl over back. Docked or undocked.

Coat: Short, close, stiff to the touch, not long and fuzzy.

Color: All white, pied, or up to 85% color [brindle, red, or buckskin patches, if there is color on the head it should appear to be color on a white head.

Disposition: Alert, outgoing and friendly with a self-assured attitude. Some aloofness with strangers and assertiveness toward other dogs is not considered a fault.

Disqualifications:

Both types:
Dogs that are deaf or males without two testicles clearly descended.
All one color with little or no white.
Black as the main color.
Buckskin to red dogs with black mask.
[Classic-type: an even or scissors bite.]

Fault Degrees:

A cosmetic fault is one of a minor nature. A fault not specified as cosmetic has to do with structure as it relates to a working dog. In a show or other evaluation, the dog is to be penalized in direct proportion to the degree of the fault.

Any fault which is extreme should be considered a serious

fault and should be penalized appropriately.

We have not included a line drawing of a Classic-type or Standard-type American Bulldog because the drawing could not take into account the variations acceptable within the realm of the working American Bulldog.

The emphasis placed on specific types in other breed standards has led to the general disintegration of the breed concerned by eliminating individuals who might have contributed significantly to respective gene pool.

Attributes other than cosmetic listed in the standard all relate to working qualities which include but are not limited to agility, endurance, leverage, biting power and heat tolerance.

Point Breakdown for Judging

Overall: proportion 10 points
temperament 10 points
total of 20 points

Head: size and shape 10 point
muzzle 5 points
teeth 5 points
total of 20 points

Body: neck 5 points
shoulders 5 points
chest 10 points
back 10 points

hindquarters 10 points
legs 10 points
feet 5 points
tail and coat 5 points
total of 60 points

Grand Total of 100 points

Note: the distinctions made between the Classic-type and the Standard-type depict an ideal representative of their respective types for show purposes only.

A Summary of the Standard-type and Johnson-type distinctions:

In actuality, many American Bulldogs are hybrids between the Classic and Standard type. The distinctions between the two types were made to allow separate shows for Classic-types and Standard-types.

Generally the Classic-type distinction allows for a slightly larger dog and requires a slightly (1/8 to 1/4 inch undershot lower jaw, but this distinction mandates separate shows for the two types.

Websites And Contact Information

The American Kennel Club
www.akc.org.

The Kennel Club
www.thekennelclub.org.uk.

American Bulldog Association
www.american-bulldog.com

American Bulldog Rescue
www.americanbulldogresuce.org

Federation American Bulldog
www.federationab.com

The Bulldog Club of America Rescue Network
www.rescuebulldogs.org

American Bulldog EU
abeu.eu/en

ABRA - American Bulldog Registry & Archives
www.abra1st.com

Training American Bulldogs
www.yourpurebredpuppy.com/training/americanbulldogs.
html

www.littlenanley.hubpages.com/hub/American-Bulldog-
Problems

Animal Poison Control Center:

United States
(888) 426-4435

United Kingdom
020 7188 0200

Glossary

A

Abdomen – That portion of a dog's body positioned between the hindquarters and the chest is commonly referred to as the abdomen or belly.

Anal glands – Dogs have two glands positioned on either side of the anus used for territorial marking. These glands can become blocked and must then be expressed by a veterinarian or trainer.

Arm – The arm of a dog is located between the shoulder and elbow. This region may also be referred to as the "upper arm."

B

Back – A dog's back extends from the shoulder or withers to the area where the back flows into the tail, called the croup.

Backyard breeder – Backyard breeders are casual or hobby breeders of purebred dogs, but they do not craft an organized breeding program with an eye toward perfecting genetic quality or meeting the set standards of the published breed standard.

Bitch – A female dog.

Blooded – A pedigreed dog.

Breed – A specifically selected and cultivated race or line of dogs bred from a common gene pool for the purpose of consistently maintaining a set of characteristics relative to appearance, function, and temperament.

Breed standard – A written document laying out the specifications a dog must meet to be regarded as a perfect representative of his breed. This includes elements relative to appearance, movement, and behavior. Breed standards are formulated by or approved by a parent canine organization, for example, the American Kennel Club or in Great Britain, The Kennel Club.

Brindle - A pattern or a marking with a pattern described in conjunction with another color. The effect is one of layering darker hairs over a lighter pattern to create a tiger striping. The combinations are black on fawn, brown, or gray.

Brows – The frontal bones forming the ridges over a dog's eyes, specifically, the contouring that creates a distinct protruberance analogous to human eyebrows.

Buttocks – A dog's rump or hips.

C

Castrate – The surgical removal of a male dog's testicles to render the animal sterile and thus incapable of reproduction.

Chest – The portion of a dog's body or trunk that is encased or protected by the ribs.

Coat – The hair covering a dog, typically comprised of an outer coat and an undercoat.

Come into Season – The colloquial term for the point in a female dog's cycle of fertility when she is capable of conceiving a litter of puppies.

Congenital – The term "congenital" refers to qualities or genetic abnormalities present at birth.

Crate – A crate is any container used to transport or temporarily house a dog. When a crate is employed in the home setting, the dog regards the space as his "den."

D

Dam – A dam is the female in a mated pair of dogs.

Dew Claw – The extra claw on the inside of a dog's leg that is a rudimentary fifth toe is called the dew claw.

E

Euthanize – Euthanasia refers to the practice of inducing a humane death, typically by means of an overdose of anesthesia, to relieve the suffering of a fatally ill or injured animal.

F

Free Feeding – Free feeding refers to making a constant supply of food freely available for a dog's consumption. It is not recommended with American Bulldogs.

G

Groom – Grooming refers to brushing, combing, trimming or any other maintenance chore intended to keep the dog and his coat clean and healthy.

H

Harness - A harness is comprised of leather or cloth straps configured to fit the shoulders and chest of a dog. Harnesses are outfitted with an upper ring to which a lead may be attached and are a popular alternative to using a dog collar.

Haunch Bones – The haunch bones are a dog's hip bones.

Haw – The haw or third eyelid is the membrane inside the corner of a dog's eye.

Head – A dog's head is comprised of the cranium and muzzle.

Hip Dysplasia – Hip dysplasia is a condition in dogs caused by a malformation of the ball and socket joint that results in varying degrees of pain and limited mobility.

Hindquarters – A dog's hindquarters are the animal's pelvis, thighs, hocks, and paws.

Hock – The hock is made up of the bones of the hind leg

forming the joint between the second thigh and the metatarsus. Also called the "true heel."

K

Kennel – A kennel is a facility where dogs are housed either for purposes of breeding or boarding.

L

Lead – A lead is any chain, cord, or strap used to restrain or lead a dog. Typically, a lead or leash is attached to a ring on a collar or harness.

Litter – A litter refers to a puppy or puppies from a single birth or "whelping."

M

Muzzle – The muzzle is the portion of a dog's head that lies in front of the eyes. It's made up of the nasal bone, nostrils, and jaws.

N

Neuter – Neutering is the surgical castration or spaying of a dog for purposes of sterilization.

P

Pedigree – A dog's pedigree is a written record of the animal's genealogy extending back three or more generations.

Puppy – A puppy is dog of less than 12 months of age.

Puppy Mill – A puppy mill is an establishment that exists to produce the maximum number of puppies for the greatest amount of profit in the least amount of time. Such operations are profit drive only and give no consideration to potential genetic defects or even basic health care.

Prey Drive – The instinctual urge felt by carnivores, or in the case of dogs, omnivores, to chase and pursue prey.

S

Separation Anxiety – Separation anxiety refers to the stress and nervousness suffered by a dog left alone for any period of time.

Sire – The sire is the male in a mated pair of dogs.

Spay – The surgical removal of a female dog's ovaries for purposes of sterilization.

W

Whelping – Whelping is the term for a female dog giving birth to puppies.

Withers – A dog's withers are the highest point of the body at the shoulders.

Wrinkle – A wrinkle is any folding or loose skin on the forehead and foreface of a dog.

Index